BLESSED BE GOD!

Psalms and Prayers
FROM
Children's Daily Prayer
FOR THE
Classroom and Home

Elizabeth McMahon Jeep

Liturgy Training Publications

Acknowledgments

Excerpts from the English translation of *A Book of Prayers,* copyright © 1982, International Committee on English in the Liturgy, Inc. (ICEL); quotations from Psalms 8, 18, 23, 27, 65, 95, 118, 121, 130, 145, 146, Canticle of Daniel, Canticle of Mary and Canticle of Zechariah from the *Liturgical Psalter,* copyright © 1993, ICEL. All rights reserved.

The English translation of the Glory to the Father by the International Consultation on English Texts (ICET).

At Table During Advent and *Blessings on Birthdays* are taken from *Catholic Household Blessings and Prayers,* copyright © 1988 by the United States Catholic Conference, Washington, D.C. 20017, and are used with permission. All rights reserved.

BLESSED BE GOD! © 1994,
Archdiocese of Chicago. All rights reserved.

 Liturgy Training Publications
1800 North Hermitage Avenue
Chicago IL 60622-1101

Order phone: 1-800-933-1800
Editorial phone: 1-312-486-8970
FAX: 1-800-933-7094

Illustrator: Suzanne M. Novak
Designer: Martinez Partners
Editor: Peter Mazar

The layout of this book is based on LTP's annual book *Children's Daily Prayer,* which was designed by Mary Bowers and revised by Kerry Perlmutter.

ISBN 1-56854-053-1
BBGCDP
$2.00

AN INTRODUCTION TO *BLESSED BE GOD*

This book contains psalms and prayers to use during the seasons of the church's year. Each season or month has its own set of prayers: a psalm, a prayer for meal times, and another prayer for the end of the day. On the last pages there are prayers for times of sadness or trouble, prayers for the dead, and a blessing for birthdays.

The pages of this book have been taken from *Children's Daily Prayer,* a larger book also published by Liturgy Training Publications. That book contains additional prayers, scripture readings and occasional blessings for each day of the school year. It is designed to be used by groups of children, especially children in a parochial school or after-school religion class.

Blessed Be God can be used by each student so that all can participate more fully in the prayers in *Children's Daily Prayer* that recur each day. Giving *Blessed Be God* to each student saves the teacher from having to make copies of various prayers during the year. While the two books are designed to work together, either can be used alone.

Children's Daily Prayer is used by many families. But even if families do not have it, they still can use *Blessed Be God*. The psalm might be said together in the morning or at any time during the day when the family is able to gather. Having prayers for mealtime and the end of the day that reflect the season can help children learn some of the rich variety of Catholic prayer.

Repeating the same prayers many times helps us learn them by heart. They become old friends. Some of these prayers may sound new to parents and teachers who memorized them many years ago. They are taken from new translations approved by the Catholic bishops of the United States.

As you can see, the prayers in *Blessed Be God* are marked so that a LEADER can guide the group. At a certain age children are able to take the part of leader. They can also participate by giving the blessing or lighting the candle when that is called for. With a little practice, everything will go smoothly.

The psalms are marked so that groups may be divided. Half of the community would read the parts marked SIDE A; the other half would read the parts marked SIDE B. A family or other small group can ignore this and have everyone read the entire psalm together. Experiment with this book and find a pattern that is best for you. You may need several copies of this book so that everyone can take their part comfortably.

This book should last a long time if it is handled carefully. Keep it in a special place so that it is easy to find when it is needed.

— *Elizabeth McMahon Jeep*

Contents

Autumn Ordinary Time

SEPTEMBER
- 6 **Psalm 145:** *Great Is the Lord*
- 7 **Meal Prayer**
- 8 **End of the Day Prayer**

OCTOBER
- 9 **Psalm:** *The Canticle of the Three Children*
- 10 **Meal Prayer:** *The Angelus*
- 11 **End of the Day Prayer:** *Prayer of St. Francis*

NOVEMBER
- 12 **Psalm 65:** *Praise Is Yours*
- 13 **Meal Prayer**
- 14 **End of the Day Prayer**

Advent

- 15 **Psalm:** *The Canticle of Zechariah*
- 16 **Meal Prayer**
- 17 **End of the Day Prayer**

Christmastime

- 18 **Psalm 98:** *Sing to the Lord a New Song*
- 19 **Meal Prayer**
- 20 **End of the Day Prayer**

Winter Ordinary Time

JANUARY
- 21 **Psalm 8:** *Lord Our God, the Whole World Tells*
- 22 **Meal Prayer**
- 23 **End of the Day Prayer**

FEBRUARY
- 24 **Psalm 146:** *Praise the Lord, My Heart*
- 25 **Meal Prayer**
- 26 **End of the Day Prayer:** *Psalm 121*

Calendar

ADVENT is the season of preparation for Christmastime, lasting from the fourth Sunday before Christmas until Christmas Eve:
November 27, 1994, to December 24, 1994
December 3, 1995, to December 24, 1995
December 1, 1996, to December 24, 1996
November 30, 1997, to December 24, 1997
November 29, 1998, to December 24, 1998

CHRISTMASTIME is the season in celebration of the coming of the Lord. The Christmas season lasts from the Birth to the Baptism of the Lord:
December 25, 1994, to January 9, 1995
December 25, 1995, to January 8, 1996
December 25, 1996, to January 12, 1997
December 25, 1997, to January 11, 1998
December 25, 1998, to January 10, 1999

Contents

Lent

EARLY LENT   From Ash Wednesday until the Fourth Sunday
- **27**   **Psalm 18:** *I Love You, God My Strength*
- **28**   **Meal Prayer**
- **29**   **End of the Day Prayer:** *The Canticle of Mary*

LATE LENT   From the Fourth Sunday until Holy Thursday afternoon
- **30**   **Psalm 130:** *From the Depths I Call to You*
- **31**   **Meal Prayer**
- **32**   **End of the Day Prayer:** *The Confiteor*

Paschal Triduum

- **33**   **A Prayer for the Paschal Triduum**

Eastertime

EARLY EASTERTIME   From Easter Sunday until April 30
- **34**   **Psalm 118:** *Give Thanks, the Lord Is Good*
- **35**   **Meal Prayer**
- **36**   **End of the Day Prayer**

LATE EASTERTIME   From May 1 until Pentecost
- **37**   **Psalm 23:** *The Lord Is My Shepherd*
- **38**   **Meal Prayer:** *The Regina Caeli*
- **39**   **End of the Day Prayer:** *Come, Holy Spirit*

Summer Ordinary Time

EARLY SUMMER   From Pentecost until mid-summer
- **40**   **Psalm 104:** *I Will Bless You, Lord My God*
- **41**   **Meal Prayer**
- **42**   **End of the Day Prayer**

LATE SUMMER   From mid-summer until the school year begins
- **43**   **Psalm 95:** *Come, Sing with Joy to God*
- **44**   **Meal Prayer**
- **45**   **End of the Day Prayer**

- **46**   **Prayers for Sad Days**
- **47**   **Prayer for the Dead**
- **48**   **Blessing for Birthdays**

Calendar

LENT is the 40-day season of preparation for the Paschal Triduum. Lent lasts from Ash Wednesday until Holy Thursday:
March 1, 1995, to April 13, 1995
February 21, 1996, to April 4, 1996
February 12, 1997, to March 27, 1997
February 25, 1998, to April 9, 1998
February 17, 1999, to April 1, 1999

The PASCHAL TRIDUUM is the 3-day season in celebration of the death, burial and resurrection of the Lord. The Triduum lasts from Holy Thursday evening until Easter Sunday afternoon:
April 13, 1995, to April 16, 1995
April 4, 1996, to April 7, 1996
March 27, 1997, to March 30, 1997
April 9, 1998, to April 12, 1998
April 1, 1999, to April 4, 1999

EASTERTIME is the 50-day season in celebration of the resurrection and ascension of the Lord and of the sending of the Holy Spirit. The Easter season lasts from Easter Sunday until Pentecost:
April 16, 1995, to June 4, 1995
April 7, 1996, to May 26, 1996
March 30, 1997, to May 18, 1997
April 12, 1998, to May 31, 1998
April 4, 1999, to May 23, 1999

A Psalm for September

 all make the sign of the cross

LEADER Great is the Lord, highly to be praised.
ALL **Age to age proclaims your works.**

SIDE A I will exalt you, God my king,
for ever bless your name.
I will bless you every day,
for ever praise your name.

SIDE B Gracious and merciful is the Lord,
slow to anger, full of love.
The Lord is good in every way,
merciful to every creature.

SIDE A The Lord is faithful in every word
and gracious in every work.
The Lord supports the fallen,
raises those bowed down.

SIDE B The Lord is just in every way,
loving in every deed.
The Lord is near to those who call,
who cry out from their hearts.

LEADER Great is the Lord, highly to be praised.
ALL **Age to age proclaims your works.**

**Glory to the Father, and to the Son,
and to the Holy Spirit:**
as it was in the beginning, is now,
    and will be for ever. Amen. Alleluia.

Psalm 145:1 – 4, 8 – 9, 13 – 14, 17 – 18

MEAL PRAYER FOR SEPTEMBER

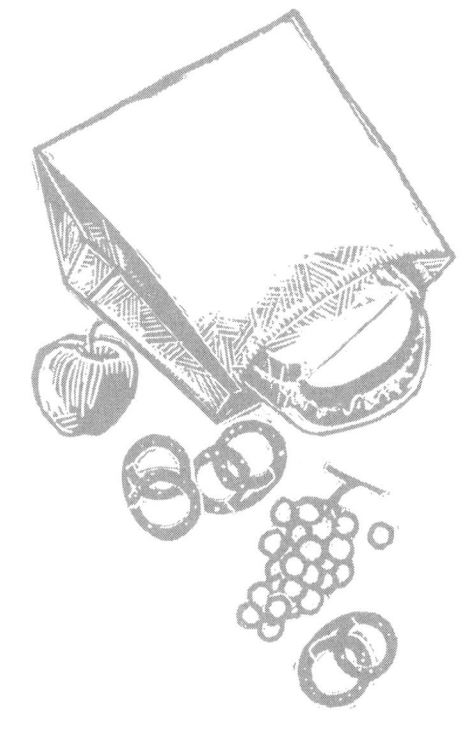

LEADER Let us offer God praise and thanksgiving:

ALL 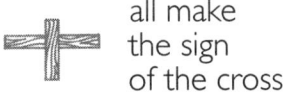 all make the sign of the cross:

In the name of the Father, and of the Son, and of the Holy Spirit. Amen.

LEADER Loving God,
    you set a table before us
    and fill it with good things.
  Teach us to share what we have
    so that no one who comes to eat
    finds an empty table.
  We ask this through Christ our Lord.

ALL **Amen.**

LEADER For the food we are about to eat
    and for the life that it nourishes,
    let us offer thanks to God:

ALL 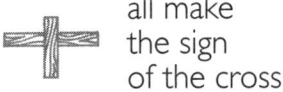 all make the sign of the cross:

In the name of the Father, and of the Son, and of the Holy Spirit. Amen.

END OF THE DAY PRAYER FOR SEPTEMBER

ALL  all make
the sign
of the cross:

**In the name of the Father, and of the Son,
and of the Holy Spirit. Amen.**

LEADER Be our shining light, O Lord,
during the rest of this day
and all through the night.
Show us the good that surrounds us
so that we might praise you.
Protect us from all dangers
that we might give you thanks through Jesus,
who is Lord for ever and ever.

ALL **Amen.**

LEADER hold out one hand
toward everyone
in blessing, and say:

May the Lord bless us,
protect us from all evil,
and bring us to everlasting life:

ALL  all make
the sign
of the cross:

**In the name of the Father, and of the Son,
and of the Holy Spirit. Amen.**

A Psalm for October

 all make the sign of the cross

LEADER Bless God beyond the stars.
Give praise and glory.

ALL **Bless God, heaven and earth.
Give praise and glory for ever.**

SIDE A Bless God, sun and moon.
Give praise and glory.

SIDE B Bless God, stars of heaven.
Give praise and glory for ever.

SIDE A Bless God, fire and heat.
Give praise and glory.

SIDE B Bless God, frost and sleet.
Give praise and glory for ever.

SIDE A Bless God, light and darkness.
Give praise and glory.

SIDE B Bless God, lightning and clouds.
Give praise and glory for ever.

LEADER Bless God beyond the stars.
Give praise and glory.

ALL **Bless God, heaven and earth.
Give praise and glory for ever.
Glory to the Father, and to the Son,
and to the Holy Spirit:
As it was in the beginning, is now,
and will be for ever. Amen. Alleluia.**

Daniel 3:56 – 57, 62 – 63, 66 – 67, 72 – 73

MEAL PRAYER FOR OCTOBER

LEADER   Let us offer God praise and thanksgiving:
ALL    all make the sign of the cross

LEADER   The angel spoke God's message to Mary,
         and she conceived of the Holy Spirit.
ALL   **Hail Mary, full of grace,
         the Lord is with you!
         Blessed are you among women,
         and blessed is the fruit of your womb, Jesus.
         Holy Mary, Mother of God,
         pray for us sinners,
         now and at the hour of our death. Amen.**

LEADER   "I am the lowly servant of the Lord:
         let it be done to me according to your word."
ALL   **Hail Mary, full of grace…**

LEADER   And the Word became flesh and lived among us.
ALL   **Hail Mary, full of grace…**

LEADER   Pray for us, holy Mother of God:
ALL   **That we may become worthy
         of the promises of Christ.**

LEADER   Let us pray.
         Lord, fill our hearts with your grace:
         once, through the message of an angel
         you revealed to us the incarnation of your Son;
         now, through his suffering and death
         lead us to the glory of his resurrection.
         We ask this through Christ our Lord.
ALL   **Amen.**

          all make the sign of the cross

END OF THE DAY PRAYER FOR OCTOBER

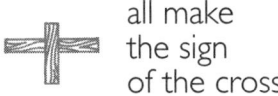 all make
the sign
of the cross

LEADER Lord, make me an instrument of your peace:

SIDE A Where there is hatred, let me sow love;
    where there is injury, pardon;
    where there is doubt, faith.

SIDE B Where there is despair, hope;
    where there is darkness, light;
    where there is sadness, joy.

SIDE A O divine Master,
    grant that I may not so much seek
      to be consoled as to console,
      to be understood as to understand,
      to be loved as to love.

SIDE B For it is in giving that we receive,
    it is in pardoning that we are pardoned,
    it is in dying that we are born
      to eternal life.

LEADER   hold out one hand
toward everyone
in blessing, and say:

May the almighty and merciful God
    bless and protect us:

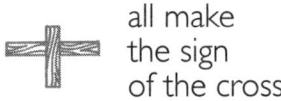 all make
the sign
of the cross

The Prayer of Saint Francis

A Psalm for November

 all make
the sign
of the cross

LEADER Blessed be the name of the Lord:
ALL **Now and for ever.**

LEADER Praise is yours, God in Zion.
ALL **Fill us with the plenty of your house.**

SIDE A You tend and water the land.
How wonderful the harvest!

SIDE B You fill your springs,
ready the seeds, prepare the grain.

SIDE A With softening rain
you bless the land with growth.

SIDE B You crown the year with riches.
All you touch comes alive.

LEADER Praise is yours, God in Zion.
ALL **Fill us with the plenty of your house.**

**Glory to the Father, and to the Son,
and to the Holy Spirit:
As it was in the beginning, is now,
and will be for ever. Amen. Alleluia.**

Psalm 65:2, 5, 10 – 12

Meal Prayer for November

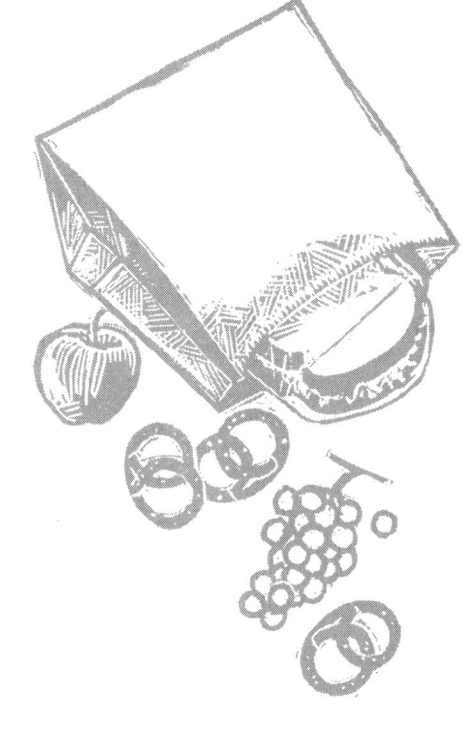

LEADER   Let us offer God praise and thanksgiving:

ALL   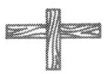 all make
the sign
of the cross

LEADER   Blessed be the name of the Lord:
ALL   **Now and for ever.**

LEADER   Loving God,
    all that we have comes from your goodness
    and the work of those who love us.
Bless us and the food we share.
Watch over those who care for us.
Open our eyes to the needs of the poor
    during this time of harvest and thanksgiving.
We make our prayer in the name of Jesus,
    who is Lord for ever and ever.

ALL   **Amen.**

♩♩♩♩ the melody for this song
is found in many hymnals:

**Now thank we all our God
  with hearts and hands and voices,
Who wondrous things has done,
  in whom this world rejoices;
Who, from our mother's arms,
  has blessed us on our way
With countless gifts of love,
  and still is ours today. Amen.**

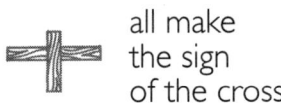 all make
the sign
of the cross

END OF THE DAY PRAYER FOR NOVEMBER

 all make the sign of the cross

LEADER Blessed be the name of the Lord:
ALL **Now and for ever.**

LEADER May all the saints look after us
  and lead us safely home.
  May they guide our steps in goodness,
    befriend us in loneliness,
    refresh us in weariness,
    and strengthen us in danger.
  We ask this in the name of Jesus,
    who is our Way, our Truth and our Life,
    now and for ever.

ALL **Amen.**

LEADER   hold out one hand toward everyone in blessing, and say:

May the almighty and merciful God
  bless and protect us:

 all make the sign of the cross

A Psalm for Advent

 all make
the sign
of the cross

 light the candles of the Advent wreath:
the first week: one (purple) candle
the second week: two (purple) candles
the third week: three candles
(one rose and two purple)
the final week: all four candles

LEADER Praise the Lord, the God of Israel,
who shepherds the people and sets them free.

ALL **God raises from David's house
a child with power to save.**

SIDE A Through the holy prophets,
God promised in ages past
to save us from enemy hands,
from the grip of all who hate us.

SIDE B Out of God's deepest mercy
a dawn will come from on high,
light for those shadowed by death,
guide for our feet on the way to peace.

LEADER Praise the Lord, the God of Israel,
who shepherds the people and sets them free.

ALL **God raises from David's house
a child with power to save.**

**Glory to the Father, and to the Son,
and to the Holy Spirit:
as it was in the beginning, is now,
and will be for ever. Amen. Alleluia.**

 at the end of prayer,
blow out the candle(s)

The Canticle of Zechariah: Luke 1:68 – 71, 78 – 79

Meal Prayer for Advent

LEADER Let us offer God praise and thanksgiving:
ALL 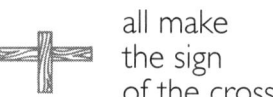 all make the sign of the cross

LEADER Come, Lord Jesus!
ALL **Come quickly!**

LEADER Blessed are you, Lord, God of all creation:
  in the darkness and in the light.

  Blessed are you
  in this food and in our sharing.

  Blessed are you as we wait in joyful hope
  for the coming of our Savior, Jesus Christ.

  For the kingdom, the power
  and the glory are yours,
  now and for ever.
ALL **Amen.**

   all make the sign of the cross

From *Catholic Household Blessings and Prayers*

END OF THE DAY PRAYER FOR ADVENT

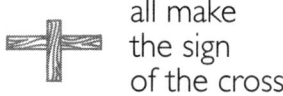 all make
the sign
of the cross

LEADER In the quiet waiting of Advent,
  let us pray to the Lord.

 stop; allow a minute or so of silence, and then say:

God of the promise, listen to our prayers.
Be with us through this evening
  and through the night.
Be close to us in our fears
  and in our hopes,
  and bring us to the brightness of morning.
We ask this in the name of Jesus the Lord.

ALL **Amen.**

♩♩♩♩ the following words can be sung to the melody for "Creator of the stars of night" or "Praise God from whom all blessings flow":

**All praise, eternal Son, to thee
Whose advent sets thy people free;
Whom with the Father we adore
And Holy Spirit ever more.**

LEADER Come, Lord Jesus!
ALL **Come quickly!**

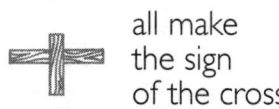 all make
the sign
of the cross

A Psalm for Christmastime

 all make the sign of the cross

LEADER Rise up in splendor, Jerusalem!
ALL **The glory of the Lord shines upon you.**

 light a candle, and then say:

LEADER God's holy day has dawned for us at last.
ALL **Come, all you peoples, and adore the Lord.**

SIDE A Sing to the Lord a new song,
the Lord of wonderful deeds.
Right hand and holy arm
brought victory to God.

SIDE B God made that victory known,
revealed justice to nations,
remembered a merciful love
loyal to the house of Israel.

ALL **The ends of the earth have seen
the victory of our God.**

LEADER God's holy day has dawned for us at last.
ALL **Come, all you peoples, and adore the Lord.**

**Glory to the Father, and to the Son,
and to the Holy Spirit:
as it was in the beginning, is now,
and will be for ever. Amen. Alleluia.**

 at the end of prayer, blow out the candle

Psalm 98:1 – 3

Meal Prayer for Christmastime

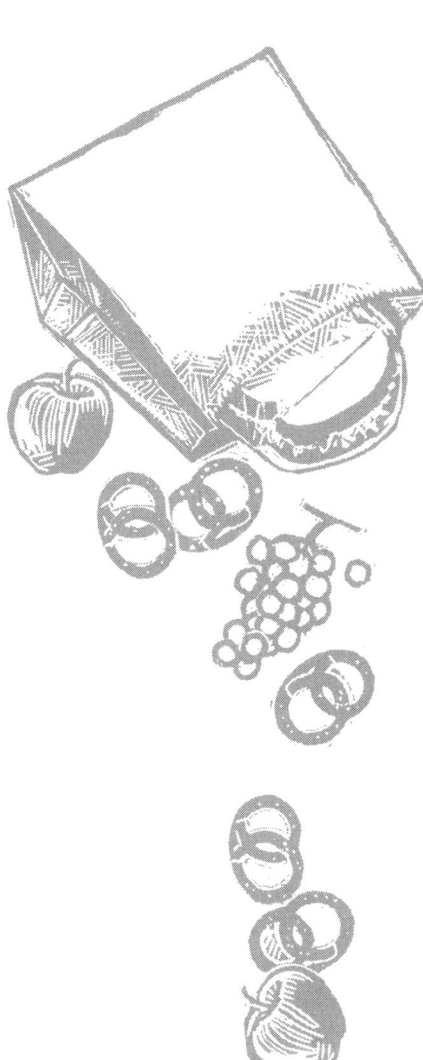

LEADER   Let us offer God praise and thanksgiving:

ALL    all make the sign of the cross

LEADER   Rise up in splendor, Jerusalem!
ALL   **The glory of the Lord shines upon you.**

LEADER   God's holy day has dawned for us at last.
ALL   **Come, all you peoples, and adore the Lord.**

**Bless us, O Lord, and these your gifts
  which we are about to receive
    from your bounty.
Through Christ our Lord. Amen.**

 all make the sign of the cross

END OF THE DAY PRAYER FOR CHRISTMASTIME

 all make
the sign
of the cross

LEADER   Rise up in splendor, Jerusalem!
ALL   **The glory of the Lord shines upon you.**

 light a candle,
and then say:

LEADER   The angels rejoiced at the coming of Jesus.
We, too, rejoice. And we sing:

 use music from the liturgy
or the refrain from a Christmas carol
to sing this response:

ALL   **Glory to God in the highest,
and peace to God's people on earth.**

LEADER   The shepherds came to worship Jesus.
We, too, worship Jesus. And we sing:
ALL   **Glory to God…**

LEADER   The Magi offered good gifts to Jesus.
We, too, bring gifts to Jesus. And we sing:
ALL   **Glory to God…**

LEADER    hold out one hand
toward everyone
in blessing, and say:

May the light of Christ shine through us
for others:

 all make
the sign
of the cross

 at the end of prayer,
blow out the candle

A Psalm for January

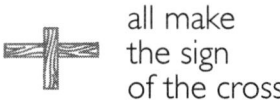 all make the sign of the cross

LEADER   Lord our God, the whole world tells
the greatness of your name.
ALL   **Your glory reaches beyond the farthest star.**

SIDE A   I see your handiwork
in the heavens:
the moon and the stars
you set in place.

SIDE B   What is humankind
that you remember them,
the human race
that you care for them?

SIDE A   You treat them like gods,
dressing them in glory and splendor.
You give them charge of the earth,
laying all at their feet:

SIDE B   Cattle and sheep,
wild beasts,
birds of the sky,
fish of the sea.

LEADER   Lord our God, the whole world tells
the greatness of your name.
ALL   **Your glory reaches beyond the farthest star.**

**Glory to the Father, and to the Son,
and to the Holy Spirit:
as it was in the beginning, is now,
and will be for ever. Amen. Alleluia.**

Psalm 8:2, 4 – 10

MEAL PRAYER FOR JANUARY

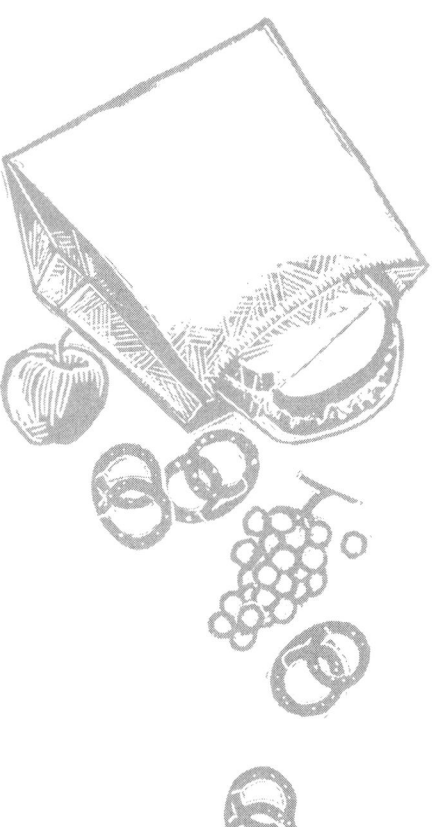

LEADER Let us offer God praise and thanksgiving:

ALL  all make
the sign
of the cross

LEADER We thank you, God, for the gift of life.
And we thank you for all that helps us grow.
Lord, we hunger for bread,
and we hunger for justice.

ALL **Lord, have mercy.**

LEADER Christ, we hunger for freedom,
and we hunger for peace.

ALL **Christ, have mercy.**

LEADER Lord, we hunger for your love,
and we hunger for your kingdom.

ALL **Lord, have mercy.**

**Bless us, O Lord, and these your gifts
which we are about to receive
from your bounty.
Through Christ our Lord. Amen.**

 all make
the sign
of the cross

End of the Day Prayer for January

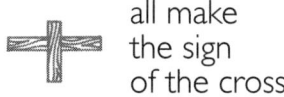 all make
the sign
of the cross

LEADER   For the circles of your universe we bless you,
      Maker of suns and seasons.

  While winter brings rest and renewal to the land,
      open our eyes every day to marvel
    at what is lovely in these weeks,
      to see also those who need shelter and warmth
      and swiftly to help them.

  In the beauty and the fierceness of winter
      be praised, our Lord, for ever and ever.

ALL   **Amen.**

LEADER   hold out one hand
toward everyone
in blessing, and say:

May the Lord bless us,
    protect us from all evil,
    and bring us to everlasting life:

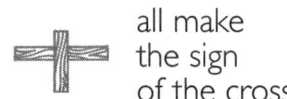 all make
the sign
of the cross

A Psalm for February

 all make the sign of the cross

LEADER Praise the Lord, my heart!
My whole life, give praise.
ALL **Let me sing to God as long as I live.**

SIDE A They are wise who depend on God,
who look to Jacob's Lord,
SIDE B creator of heaven and earth,
maker of the teeming sea.

SIDE A The Lord keeps faith for ever,
giving food to the hungry,
SIDE B justice to the poor,
freedom to captives.

SIDE A The Lord opens blind eyes
and straightens the bent,
SIDE B comforting widows and orphans,
protecting the stranger.

LEADER Praise the Lord, my heart!
My whole life, give praise.
ALL **Let me sing to God as long as I live.**

**Glory to the Father, and to the Son,
and to the Holy Spirit:
as it was in the beginning, is now,
and will be for ever. Amen. Alleluia.**

Psalm 146:1 – 2, 5 – 9

Meal Prayer for February

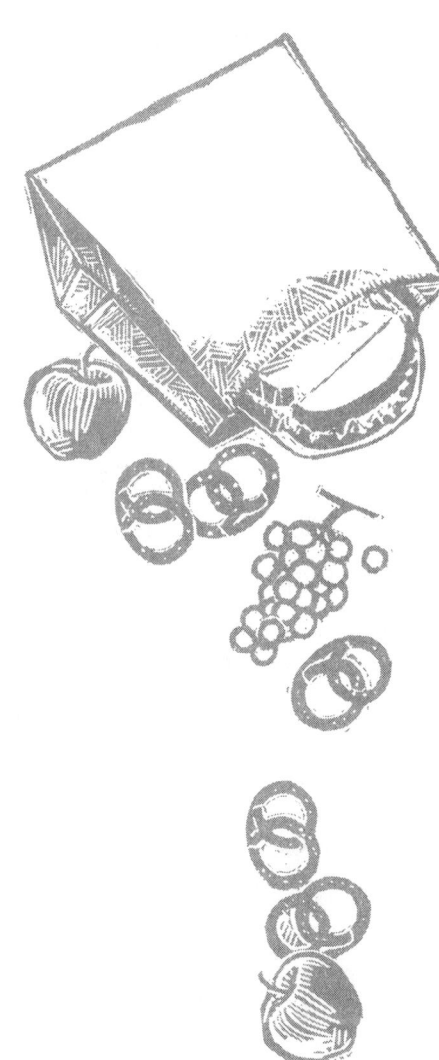

LEADER   Let us offer God praise and thanksgiving:

ALL   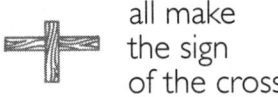 all make
the sign
of the cross

LEADER   Praise the Lord, my heart!
My whole life, give praise.

ALL   **Let me sing to God as long as I live.**

LEADER   Blessed are you, Lord:
You have fed us from our earliest days.
You give food to every living creature.

Fill our hearts with joy and delight.
Let us always have enough
   and something to spare for works of mercy
   in honor of Christ Jesus, our Lord.

Through Christ may glory, honor and power
   be yours for ever and ever.

ALL   **Amen.**

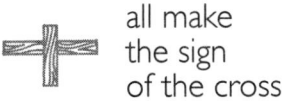 all make
the sign
of the cross

End of the Day Prayer for February

 all make
the sign
of the cross

LEADER God, come to my assistance.
ALL **Lord, make haste to help me.**

LEADER Our help is in the name of the Lord:
ALL **Who made heaven and earth.**

LEADER May God, ever wakeful,
keep you from stumbling;
the guardian of Israel
neither rests nor sleeps.

God shelters you from evil,
securing your life.
God watches over you near and far,
now and always.

 hold out one hand
toward everyone
in blessing, and say:

May the Lord bless us,
   protect us from all evil,
   and bring us to everlasting life:

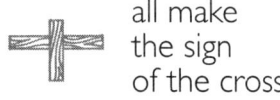 all make
the sign
of the cross

Psalm 121:2–4, 7–8

A Psalm for Early Lent

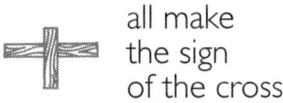 all make the sign of the cross

LEADER Behold! Now is the acceptable time!
ALL **Now is the day of salvation!**

LEADER I love you, God my strength,
ALL **my rock, my shelter, my stronghold.**

SIDE A My God, I lean on you,
my shield, my rock,
my champion, my defense.

SIDE B When I call for help,
I am safe from my enemies.

SIDE A From the depths I cried out,
my plea reached the heavens.
God heard me.

SIDE B The Lord lives!
Blessed be my rock,
the God who saves me.

LEADER I love you, God my strength,
ALL **my rock, my shelter, my stronghold.**

**Glory to the Father, and to the Son,
and to the Holy Spirit:
as it was in the beginning, is now,
and will be for ever. Amen.**

Psalm 18:2 – 4, 7, 47

Meal Prayer for Early Lent

LEADER   Let us offer God praise and thanksgiving:

ALL    all make the sign of the cross

LEADER   Behold! Now is the acceptable time!
ALL   **Now is the day of salvation!**

LEADER   I was hungry:
ALL   **And you gave me food.**

LEADER   I was thirsty:
ALL   **And you gave me drink.**

LEADER   I was a stranger:
ALL   **And you welcomed me.**

LEADER   I was naked:
ALL   **And you clothed me.**

LEADER   I was ill:
ALL   **And you cared for me.**

LEADER   I was in jail:
ALL   **And you visited me.**

LEADER   Lord Jesus Christ,
    be with all those who are in need.
Bless us,
    and bless the food we eat today.
Help our families, our school and our parish
    keep a good and holy Lent.
And bring us quickly to the glory of Easter.
We ask this through Christ our Lord.

ALL   **Amen.**

all make the sign of the cross

Matthew 25:35 – 36

End of the Day Prayer for Early Lent

 all make
the sign
of the cross

LEADER I acclaim the greatness of the Lord.
ALL **I delight in God my savior.**

SIDE A Truly from this day on
all ages will call me blest.
For God, wonderful in power,
has used that strength for me.

SIDE B Holy the name of the Lord!
whose mercy embraces the faithful,
one generation to the next.

SIDE A The Lord fills the starving
and lets the rich go hungry.

SIDE B God rescues lowly Israel,
recalling the promise of mercy,
the promise made to our ancestors,
to Abraham's heirs for ever.

LEADER I acclaim the greatness of the Lord.
ALL **I delight in God my savior.**

LEADER   hold out one hand
toward everyone
in blessing, and say:

May the almighty and merciful God
bless and protect us:

 all make
the sign
of the cross

The Canticle of Mary: Luke 1:46 – 50, 53 – 54

A Psalm for Late Lent

 all make the sign of the cross

LEADER Behold! Now is the acceptable time!
ALL **Now is the day of salvation!**

LEADER From the depths I call to you,
Lord, hear my cry.
ALL **Catch the sound of my voice
raised up, pleading.**

SIDE B If you record our sins,
Lord, who could survive?
But because you forgive
we stand in awe.

SIDE A I trust in God's word,
I trust in the Lord.
More than sentries for dawn
I watch for the Lord.

SIDE B More than sentries for dawn
let Israel watch.
The Lord will bring mercy
and grant full pardon.

LEADER From the depths I call to you,
Lord, hear my cry.
ALL **Catch the sound of my voice
raised up, pleading.**

**Glory to the Father, and to the Son,
and to the Holy Spirit:
as it was in the beginning, is now,
and will be for ever. Amen.**

Psalm 130:1 – 7

Meal Prayer for Late Lent

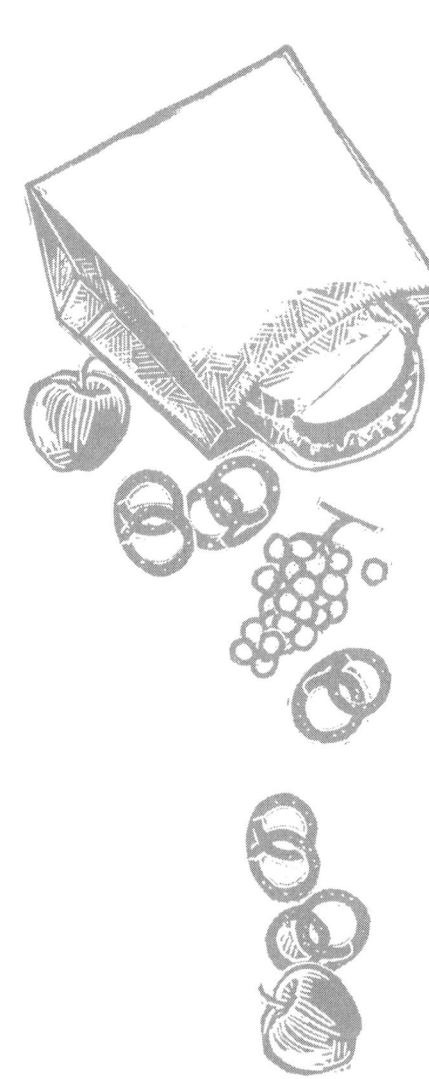

LEADER   Let us offer God praise and thanksgiving:

ALL   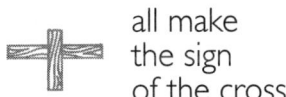 all make
the sign
of the cross

LEADER   Behold! Now is the acceptable time!
ALL   **Now is the day of salvation!**

LEADER   Blessed are you, Lord, God of all creation:
ALL   **You make us hunger and thirst for holiness.**

LEADER   Blessed are you, Lord, God of all creation:
ALL   **You call us to true fasting:**
      to set free the oppressed,
      to share our bread with the hungry,
      and to shelter the homeless.

LEADER   May your gifts refresh us, O Lord,
      and your grace give us strength.

    ✝ all make
the sign
of the cross

END OF THE DAY PRAYER FOR LATE LENT

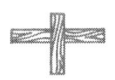 all make
the sign
of the cross

LEADER Let us look back over our day
and ask forgiveness
for anything we did that was harmful or wrong.

 stop; allow a minute or so of silence,
and then say:

LEADER To you, O Lord, I lift up my soul.
ALL **In you, my God, I put my trust.**

**I confess to almighty God,
and to you, my brothers and sisters,
that I have sinned through my own fault
in my thoughts and in my words,
in what I have done,
and in what I have failed to do;
and I ask blessed Mary, every virgin,
all the angels and saints,
and you, my brothers and sisters,
to pray for me to the Lord our God.**

LEADER   hold out one hand
toward everyone
in blessing, and say:

May the almighty and merciful God
bless and protect us:

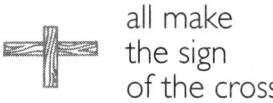 all make
the sign
of the cross

32   The Confiteor

A Prayer for the Paschal Triduum

 all make the sign of the cross

LEADER We worship you, Lord,
  we venerate your cross,
  we praise your resurrection.

ALL **Through the cross you brought joy
  to the world.**

LEADER For our sake Christ was obedient,
  accepting even death, death on a cross.

  Therefore God raised him on high
  and gave him the name
  above all other names.

  Holy God!

ALL **Holy God!**

LEADER Holy mighty One!
ALL **Holy mighty One!**

LEADER Holy immortal One, have mercy on us!
ALL **Holy immortal One, have mercy on us!**

LEADER We worship you, Lord,
  we venerate your cross,
  we praise your resurrection.

ALL **Through the cross you brought joy
  to the world.**

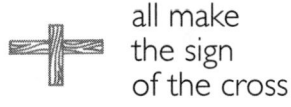 all make the sign of the cross

A Psalm for Early Eastertime

 all make the sign of the cross

LEADER Christ is risen like the sun, alleluia!
ALL **The light of Christ shines
over the whole world, alleluia!**

 light a candle, and then say:

LEADER This is the day the Lord made.
ALL **Let us rejoice and be glad.**

SIDE A Give thanks, the Lord is good,
"God is lasting love!"
Now let Israel say,
"God is lasting love!"

SIDE B I was pushed to falling,
but the Lord gave me help.
My strength, my song is the Lord,
who has become my savior.

SIDE A The stone the builders rejected
has become the cornerstone.

SIDE B This is the work of the Lord,
how wonderful in our eyes.

LEADER This is the day the Lord made.
ALL **Let us rejoice and be glad.**

**Glory to the Father, and to the Son,
and to the Holy Spirit:
as it was in the beginning, is now,
and will be for ever. Amen. Alleluia.**

 at the end of prayer, blow out the candle

Psalm 118:1 – 2, 13 – 14, 22 – 24

Meal Prayer for Early Eastertime

LEADER Let us offer God praise and thanksgiving:

ALL ✝ all make
the sign
of the cross

LEADER Christ is risen, alleluia!
ALL **Christ is truly risen, alleluia!**

LEADER Jesus says to us:
"I am the living bread
that came down from heaven.
Whoever eats of this bread will live forever."

ALL **Loving God, give us the daily bread
that is your Son, Jesus,
who is our resurrection and our life,
now and for ever. Amen.**

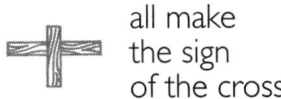 the melody for this song
is found in many hymnals:

**I am the Bread of life.
You who come to me shall not hunger
and who believe in me shall not thirst.
No one can come to me
unless the Father beckons.**

**And I will raise you up,
and I will raise you up,
and I will raise you up
on the last day.**

 all make
the sign
of the cross

John 6

END OF THE DAY PRAYER FOR EARLY EASTERTIME

 all make
the sign
of the cross

LEADER Christ is risen like the sun, alleluia!
ALL **The light of Christ shines
over the whole world, alleluia!**

 light a candle,
and then say:

LEADER Loving God, Creator of the universe,
    we thank you for calling us
        to be members of your holy people, and we say:
ALL **Amen.**

LEADER Lord Jesus Christ,
    we thank you for forgiving our sins
        and for sharing with us your risen life, and we say:
ALL **Amen.**

LEADER Holy Spirit of God,
    fill us with your love
        and guide us in the way of peace, and we say:
ALL **Amen.**

LEADER  hold out one hand
toward everyone
in blessing, and say:

Wherever we go,
    may we live in the light of Christ:

 all make
the sign
of the cross

 at the end of prayer,
blow out the candle

A Psalm for Late Eastertime

 all make
the sign
of the cross

LEADER   Christ is risen like the sun, alleluia!
ALL   **The light of Christ shines
over the whole world, alleluia!**

 light a candle,
and then say:

LEADER   The Lord is my shepherd, all that I need,
giving me rest in green and pleasant fields,
ALL   **reviving my life by finding fresh water,
guiding my ways with a shepherd's care.**

SIDE A   Though I should walk in death's dark valley,
I fear no evil with you by my side.
Your shepherd's staff comforts me.

SIDE B   You spread my table in sight of my foes,
anoint my head, my cup runs over.
You tend me with love always loyal.
I dwell with you, Lord, as long as I live.

LEADER   The Lord is my shepherd, all that I need,
giving me rest in green and pleasant fields,
ALL   **reviving my life by finding fresh water,
guiding my ways with a shepherd's care.**

**Glory to the Father, and to the Son,
and to the Holy Spirit:
as it was in the beginning, is now,
and will be for ever. Amen. Alleluia.**

at the end of prayer,
blow out the candle

Psalm 23:1 – 6

Meal Prayer for Late Eastertime

LEADER Let us offer God praise and thanksgiving:

ALL  all make the sign of the cross

LEADER Christ is risen, alleluia!
ALL **Christ is truly risen, alleluia!**

LEADER O Queen of heaven, rejoice:
ALL **Alleluia.**

LEADER For he to whom you once gave birth:
ALL **Alleluia.**

LEADER Has risen as he promised:
ALL **Alleluia.**

LEADER Pray for us to God:
ALL **Alleluia.**

LEADER Rejoice and be glad, O Virgin Mary, alleluia.
ALL **For the Lord has truly risen, alleluia.**

LEADER God, through the resurrection of your Son,
    our Lord Jesus Christ,
      you gave joy to the world.
  Now through the prayer of his mother,
    the Virgin Mary,
      may we gain the joys of everlasting life.
  We ask this in the name of Jesus the Lord.
ALL **Amen.**

 all make the sign of the cross

The Regina Caeli: from *A Book of Prayers*

END OF THE DAY PRAYER FOR LATE EASTERTIME

 all make
the sign
of the cross

LEADER Christ is risen like the sun, alleluia!
ALL **The light of Christ shines
over the whole world, alleluia!**

 light a candle,
and then say:

LEADER Come, Holy Spirit,
fill the hearts of your faithful.
ALL **And kindle in them the fire of your love.**

LEADER Send forth your Spirit
and they shall be created.
ALL **And you will renew the face of the earth.**

LEADER Gracious God,
send your Spirit into the church
to strengthen the hearts of all who believe.
And send your Spirit into the world
to fulfill the work of the gospel.
We ask this through Christ our Lord.
ALL **Amen.**

LEADER  hold out one hand
toward everyone
in blessing, and say:

May we live in the light of Christ:

 all make
the sign
of the cross

 at the end of prayer,
blow out the candle

39

A Psalm for Early Summer

✝ all make the sign of the cross

LEADER Lord, open my lips.
ALL **And my mouth will proclaim your praise.**

LEADER I will bless you, Lord my God!
ALL **You fill the world with awe.**

SIDE A You dress yourself in light,
in rich, majestic light.
You drench the hills
with rain from high heaven.
You nourish the earth
with what you create.

SIDE B You make grass grow for cattle,
make plants grow for people,
food to eat from the earth
and wine to warm the heart,
oil to glisten on faces
and bread for bodily strength.

LEADER I will bless you, Lord my God!
ALL **You fill the world with awe.**

Glory to the Father, and to the Son,
  and to the Holy Spirit:
as it was in the beginning, is now,
  and will be for ever. Amen. Alleluia.

Psalm 104:1 – 2, 13 – 15

MEAL PRAYER FOR EARLY SUMMER

LEADER Let us offer God praise and thanksgiving:

ALL  all make
the sign
of the cross

LEADER Let us pray.
Lord, the lover of life,
   you feed the birds of the skies
   and dress the lilies of the field.
We bless you for all your creatures
   and for the food we are about to receive.
We humbly pray that in your goodness
   you will provide for our brothers and sisters
   who are hungry.
We ask this through Christ our Lord.

ALL **Amen.**

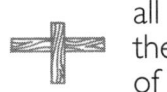 the following words
can be sung to the melody for
"Praise God from whom all blessings flow":

Be present at our table, Lord.
Be here and everywhere adored.
Thy creatures bless and grant that we
May feast in Paradise with thee. Amen.

 all make
the sign
of the cross

END OF THE DAY PRAYER FOR EARLY SUMMER

 all make
the sign
of the cross

LEADER   Let us praise and glorify God
     for the beauty of our summer world.

  For sunshine that warms the day, we pray:

ALL   **Glory to you, O Lord.**

LEADER   For rain that makes the grass sparkle, we pray:
ALL   **Glory to you, O Lord.**

LEADER   For bright mornings and free afternoons, we pray:
ALL   **Glory to you, O Lord.**

LEADER   For our good mother earth, we pray:
ALL   **Glory to you, O Lord.**

 other praises
may be added

LEADER   Lord our God, you create us out of the earth
     and ask us to care for it.

  Give us strength like your own,
     and fill us with knowledge
       that we may know the majesty of your works
       and praise your holy name.

  We ask this through Christ our Lord.

ALL   **Amen.**

LEADER   hold out one hand
toward everyone
in blessing, and say:

May the almighty and merciful God
    bless and protect us:

 all make
the sign
of the cross

A Psalm for Late Summer

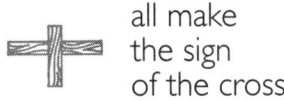 all make the sign of the cross

LEADER	Lord, open my lips.
ALL	**And my mouth will proclaim your praise.**
LEADER	Come, sing with joy to God, shout to our savior, our rock.
ALL	**Enter God's presence with praise, enter with shouting and song.**
SIDE A	God cradles the depths of the earth, holds fast the mountain peaks.
SIDE B	God shaped the ocean and owns it, formed the earth by hand.
SIDE A	Come, bow down and worship, kneel to the Lord our maker.
SIDE B	This is our God, our shepherd, we are the flock led with care.
LEADER	Come, sing with joy to God, shout to our savior, our rock.
ALL	**Enter God's presence with praise, enter with shouting and song.**
	Glory to the Father, and to the Son, and to the Holy Spirit: as it was in the beginning, is now, and will be for ever. Amen. Alleluia.

Psalm 95:1 – 2, 4 – 7

Meal Prayer for Late Summer

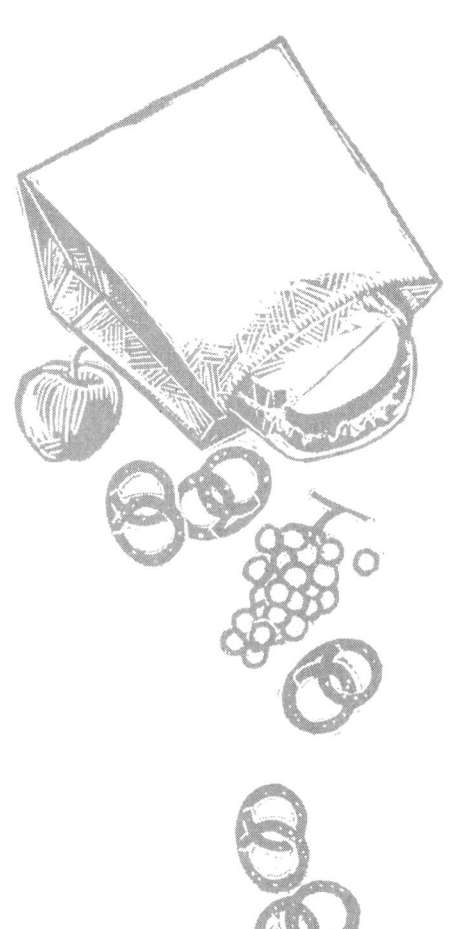

LEADER   Let us offer God praise and thanksgiving:

ALL   ✝ all make
the sign
of the cross

LEADER   All the world hopes in you, O Lord,
that you will give us food in our hunger.

ALL   You open wide your hand
and we are filled with good things.

Bless us, O Lord, and these your gifts
which we are about to receive
from your bounty.
Through Christ our Lord. Amen.

✝ all make
the sign
of the cross

END OF THE DAY PRAYER FOR LATE SUMMER

 all make
the sign
of the cross

LEADER God, come to my assistance.
ALL **Lord, make haste to help me.**

 the following words
can be sung to the melody for
"Praise God from whom all blessings flow":

**Lord, bless the work that I have done,
   and bless the evening still to come.
Let my return a blessing be
   to all who share a home with me.
Give us with food and rest and play
   a fitting end to this good day.
From webs of sin grant us release,
   and touch our planet with your peace.**

LEADER hold out one hand
toward everyone
in blessing, and say:

May the Lord bless us,
   protect us from all evil,
   and bring us to everlasting life.

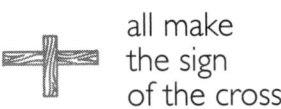 all make
the sign
of the cross

Prayers for Sad Days

 all make the sign of the cross

Psalm 18:28
O my God,
  you brighten the darkness about me.

Psalm 27:13–14
I believe that I shall see the goodness of the Lord
  in the land of the living.
Wait for the Lord.
Be strong, and let your heart take courage.
Wait for the Lord!

Isaiah 41:10
Do not fear, for I am with you.
Do not be afraid, for I am your God;
  I will strengthen you, I will help you,
  I will hold you in my hand.

Prayer

LEADER Most holy and most merciful God,
  strength of the weak,
  rest for the weary,
  comfort of the sorrowful,
  our refuge in every time of need:
Grant us strength and protect us.
Support us in all dangers,
  and carry us through all trials.
We ask this through Christ our Lord.

ALL **Amen.**

 all make the sign of the cross

Prayer for the Dead

 all make
the sign
of the cross

LEADER Blessed be God,
who raised Jesus Christ from the dead.
Let us all say: Blessed be God for ever.

ALL **Blessed be God for ever.**

LEADER In silence, let us take a few moments now
to remember the dead.

 stop; allow a minute or so of silence,
and then say:

Lord God, whose days are without end
and whose mercies beyond counting,
keep us mindful that life is short
and the hour of death unknown.

Let your Spirit guide our days on earth
in the ways of holiness and justice,
that we may serve you in union with the whole church,
sure in faith, strong in hope, perfected in love.

And when our earthly journey is ended,
lead us rejoicing into your kingdom,
where you live for ever and ever.

ALL **Amen.**

LEADER Eternal rest grant unto them, O Lord.
ALL **And let perpetual light shine upon them.**

LEADER May they rest in peace.
ALL **Amen.**

LEADER May their souls and the souls of all the faithful departed,
through the mercy of God, rest in peace.
ALL **Amen.**

 all make
the sign
of the cross

Adapted from *Catholic Household Blessings and Prayers*

Blessing for Birthdays

 all make the sign of the cross

LEADER Loving God,
   you created all the people of the world,
   and you know each of us by name.

   We thank you for **N.**,
   who celebrates his/her birthday.

   Bless him/her with your love and friendship
   that he/she may grow in wisdom,
     knowledge, and grace.

   May he/she love his/her family always
   and be ever faithful to his/her friends.

   Grant this through Christ our Lord.

ALL **Amen.**

 those present may place a hand on the head or shoulders of the person being blessed

LEADER May God, in whose presence our ancestors walked,
   bless you.

ALL **Amen.**

LEADER May God, who has been your shepherd from birth until now,
   keep you.

ALL **Amen.**

LEADER May God, who saves you from all harm,
   give you peace.

ALL **Amen.**

 all make the sign of the cross

From *Catholic Household Blessings and Prayers*